MW01103338

TWO DATES FOR THE PROM

STEVE SWANSON

CHARIOT
FAMILY PUBLISHING

TWO DATES FOR THE PROM

STEVE SWANSON

Published by Chariot Books,
an imprint of David C. Cook Publishing Co.
David C. Cook Publishing Co., Elgin, Illinois 60120
David C. Cook Publishing Co., Weston, Ontario
Nova Distribution, Ltd., Newton Abbot, England

TWO DATES FOR THE PROM
© 1993 by Steve Swanson

Cover illustration by Joe Van Severen
Cover design by Jack Foster
First printing, 1993
Printed in the United States of America
97 96 95 94 93 5 4 3 2 1

Library of Congress Cataloging-in-Publication Data
Swanson, Steve.
         Two dates for the prom/Steve Swanson.
         p.   cm.
Summary: Bible verses accompany scenarios which present
concerns and events from young people's daily lives.
ISBN 1-55513-937-X
1. Teenagers—Prayer-books and devotions—English. 2.
Spiritual life—Christianity. [1. Prayer books and devotions.
2. Christian life.]   I. Title.
BV4531.2.S86   1993
242'.63—dc20   93-6965
                                           CIP
                                           AC

Two Dates for the Prom

KEY VERSE ▶

". . . Each of you must put off falsehood and speak truthfully to his neighbor, for we are all members of one body."

EPHESIANS 4:25

Jeremy Ames had gotten burned. Everybody in school did the same dumb thing about the prom. They all said, "You have to get your date early." That was the tradition. But by the time the prom finally came, you usually wished you were going with someone else. Most guys took cold showers, bit down hard on a beach towel, and went with the girl they had first asked, no matter what.

Jeremy had asked Amber way back in February. By April their passion had cooled down some—but he would have taken her anyway. Then came the May Day picnic when Jeremy and Sarah (why hadn't he ever noticed her before?) had one of those magic moments on the footbridge over the lake.

The moon wasn't full, but it was out. The lake wasn't like glass, but it was fairly smooth. The breeze wasn't whispering through the trees. Actually there was no breeze at all, and anyway there were no trees out there on the bridge. But it was romantic. He had stood there holding Sarah's hand and thinking, *If Amber's grandma hadn't suddenly died, I'd be standing here with Amber. God forgive me, but if Amber's grandma had to die, I'm glad she chose May Day picnic weekend to do it—because HERE I AM WITH SARAH.*

Jeremy stood there wishing he had met Sarah back in February—just a day or two before he had asked Amber to the prom would have been okay. He more or less said so out loud. That's when the problem started. After they had talked in whispers for a while, Jeremy said, "I wish we were going to the prom together."

"So do I. We could, you know."

"I thought you were going with Tom."

"He broke that one. He's going with Sue."

"I thought Sue was going with Al."

"Al's going with Lisa. Except for Duane, I'm about the only one left over."

"Then we really could go together."

"But I thought you were going with Amber."

"That's not for sure," Jeremy lied.

That's how he got into it. How many times after that had Jeremy prayed, "Lord, why didn't You stop up my mouth?" Or "Lord, why didn't You call me to be a hermit when I was fifteen?" Or "Lord, why aren't my folks missionaries in Saudi Arabia—someplace where they don't date?"

Jeremy couldn't bring himself to tell either of the girls. He finally hatched an elaborate plan and he hired, he actually hired, Duane to help.

6

"Foo," he said—everyone called Duane "Foo"—
"you've got to help me." Foo had no date. Didn't
believe in them, really. He was good looking, though,
and nice, and lots of girls would gladly have gone with
him. By paying for Foo's tux and promising a week's
free gas for his pickup, Jeremy had convinced him.
They talked and argued and then together they
hatched:

THE PLAN
1. Amber lives out in the country, so Jeremy gets
   her first.
2. Jeremy and Amber arrive; Foo takes over
   Amber at the gym.
3. Jeremy picks up Sarah, a little late so the floor
   will be crowded.
4. (Remember to buy two corsages.)
5. Tell Sarah that Foo has a date with Amber.
6. Tell Amber that Foo has a date with Sarah.
7. Tell Amber that Jeremy's Grandma Ames is
   deathly sick and he needs to call home every
   twenty minutes. (After being at her own
   grandma's funeral, she should go for that one.)
8. Tell Sarah he isn't feeling well and has to go to
   the men's room every twenty minutes.
9. Keep Amber on the scoreboard end.
10 Keep Sarah on the locker room end.
11. Foo and Jeremy have to tell each other exactly
    where to find the other.
12. Don't go out on the floor unless it's crowded.
13. Arrange times to be, and not to be, at the

punch bowl.

14. Etc. etc.

It actually worked. That is, it was working well until about ten o'clock, when Jeremy's mom showed up. She had decided they should trade cars before morning. She found Foo and Amber out on the floor. (She didn't know about Sarah at all.)

Jeremy (according to Amber) had already called home three times about his sick grandmother, and indeed had only a few minutes earlier said he was leaving to try calling home again. That's why Amber was with Foo, of course.

Well, why wouldn't Amber ask Jeremy's mom about his grandma who was so very sick? And why wouldn't Jeremy's mom be totally confused?

Amber was so very soft-spoken and solicitous. "Did she die?" Amber whispered, fearing the worst. Why else would Jeremy's mom have appeared at the prom?

"You mean the car?" Mrs. Ames replied with a confused look.

"I mean your mother-in-law, Jeremy's grandma."

Well, one thing led to another. Foo confessed. Amber stomped to the locker room end of the gym and found Sarah and Jeremy. There was a noisy and, everyone said afterwards, funny confrontation. They said it was better than a soap opera. The two girls were going to leave until they thought better of it. They hunted until they found Jeremy hiding behind the punch bowl.

"We've decided we're not going to leave," Sarah said.

"No," Amber agreed.

"You leave," they said in unison, like a pair of angry, avenging angels from a Michelangelo painting. They both pointed at the door. Everyone clapped. Jeremy left; Foo stayed. For the rest of the evening the two girls treated Foo like visiting royalty, so said Foo—and that's all he'd say. They must have made some sort of deal among themselves.

Of course neither girl ever gave Jeremy so much as the time of day after that. They giggled together and pointed at him in the hallway a few times that spring, and that was it.

As he sat home and watched TV on the night of the graduation party, Jeremy remembered the prom. *That could have been the greatest feat in the history of dating,* he thought. Yes, it could have been.

Then he thought about Sarah and the footbridge and how he still thought she was great, and how he had ruined everything by lying to her. *She and I could be at the graduation party tonight,* he thought. But it was all wrong from the beginning. It began with a lie.

"I'm never going to lie to a girl again," he declared to himself.

And he didn't.

▶ Dig a little deeper:

Ephesians 4:1-6, 20-25

When You're Young

KEY VERSE ▶

*". . . Banish anxiety from
your heart and cast off the
troubles of your body, for
youth and vigor are
meaningless."*

ECCLESIASTES 11:10

Grandpa always used to say, "You do crazy things
when you're young." But I had never done anything
really crazy, nothing Gramps himself might not
have done, until this morning. At my own sister's
wedding. . . .

Jill, my sister, is ten years older than I am. That
means that for quite a few years she hasn't been
around. Like, she started college when I was eight and
really hasn't been here much since. After college she
went to teach out in the western part of the state, and
that's where she met Dan. He's a teacher too.

At her wedding this morning, I was a groomsman.
That's the third or fourth or eighth guy to the right
when the wedding party lines up at the altar. Nice of
Dan to ask me. He's okay.

It was a beautiful wedding. I mean, a January
wedding has some advantages. The candles seem

warm, and no matter how cold it is outside, it's warm in the church. When my cousin Tom was married last summer, it was 95 degrees outside—and felt like 100 in the church. Candles in summer add to the problem. I like January better—or I did until today.

In January around here, there's always snow. I don't know what I was thinking of. Everything had gone so well up until then. The preacher said some neat stuff—even got a few laughs. The ceremony was beautiful. Mom raved about the caterers. The food and the decorations for the reception were great. When the ceremony ended, everything was ready and waiting for us down in the church basement.

As we were coming out, the ushers handed us these little lacy things full of sunflower seeds. Jill and Dan, her boyfriend—I mean, her husband—were supposed to run out the front door, around the side, and into the church basement while we all chucked seeds at them.

I guess rice used to be the traditional thing, but in our church we use sunflower seeds. Mr. Hansen, our janitor, says the cardinals and jays and squirrels eat them up the next day—and the husks help make the sidewalks less slippery.

Anyway, being the sort of hang-back guy I am, I was on the fringe of the crowd. Everyone was dancing around and trying to keep warm while they waited. Some had put on coats, some had draped coats over their shoulders, and some of us crazy macho men just went out and stood there in the snow trying not to shiver.

I opened my lacy little bag of seeds and hefted them in my hand. From where I stood it would take a major-league throw to get even a few of them near the blessed couple. I mean, as a projectile, a sunflower seed is about 3 percent.

So what I did, which proved Grandpa right, was to press my seeds into some snow to make a sort of sunflower snowball. Understand, I didn't pack it hard. It wasn't like the ones we used to make after school in the sixth grade and stockpile for wars while we waited for the school bus.

No, I love my sister. I wouldn't hurt her. I wouldn't make an icy snowball or a heavy one. Not on her wedding day. I just wanted to be part of everything. Maybe I wanted to be noticed.

If I could have had my way with the snowball, it would have been as soft as cotton and arched gracefully over the heads of the crowd and glanced, just glanced off her lacy white shoulder.

She would have pretended to look and see who had thrown it, but she would have known it was me. She would have found my face beaming at her from the outer edge of the crowd. She would have smiled a warm and gentle smile that said: "I love you, Brad. I'm marrying Dan, but I still love you. You are my brother, my only brother, my very special person—and always will be."

And I would smile back, "I love you too, Jill. I wish we had been closer in age so we could have done more things together. I hope that Dan is good enough for you. If he ever treats you wrong, you just let me know—I'll fix him."

That was what I was thinking. That was what I wanted the snowball to do in my fantasy—just to get her attention. Just so we could have had that one glance, that one last moment of understanding before she went off to be a wife and mother and everything.

It didn't work out that way.

In all my winters of snowball fighting and snowball teasing and snowball heckling and who's-the-first-one-to-hit-the-yield-sign contests, I guess the best shot I ever had was when my Uncle Pete was driving away one slushy afternoon. His car windows were open the way we all do on those first spring days. He was leaning over and waving to us as he drove away. I packed a heavy one and in a center-field-to-home plate masterpiece, leading him like a duck hunter, I put it through his open window at 100 feet and ten miles per hour.

My dad said, "What a shot!" My mom, smiling, said, "Shame on you, Brad," and my Uncle Pete raised a fist over his roof and shook it—then honked twice and drove off. I knew he was laughing too. That's snowballing at its best.

But the snowball I threw at Jill was no laughing matter. I knew when it was halfway there that I had made a terrible mistake. I would have taken it back then, if I could have. But I couldn't. It hit her in the left eye. Not hard, but hard enough.

Everything stopped. They took her inside. Doc Witham was there, of course. He looked. Said her eyeball could be scratched. He went to his car, got his bag, and taped a gauze patch over her eye—to be left on overnight, just in case, he said. Some honeymoon present I gave them.

As soon as I knew she was all right, I slipped out and went across the parking lot to Whitmores' barn. I was so ashamed and sorry. I mean, how could something that was meant so well, that had so much love in it, cause so much harm and excitement and embarrassment?

I sat in the hayloft for a half hour or so, shivering. Then I heard a noise down near the calf pen and looked down. It was Gramps.

"You do crazy things when you're young," he said.

"You sure do," I said softly.

"I kind of thought you'd be here," he said. "This is where I would have come when I was your age." He smiled at me. "Come on down."

"Okay."

He brushed the straw off my tuxedo and straightened my bow tie. "Let's go back now."

I didn't argue. His arm felt warm across my shivering shoulders.

"Is Jill mad at me?"

"Of course not. Everyone knew it was an accident. Do you know what she said?" He waited for my response.

"No."

"She stood up in front of everyone and said, 'Every wedding needs a memorable moment—a moment no one will forget. I want to thank my crazy brother Brad for giving us all that moment.' She was looking for you when she said it. Everyone clapped." He turned to shut the barn door after us. "You can come back now. It's all forgiven."

"Thanks, Gramps."

"Don't mention it. You do—"

"—crazy things when you're young," I finished for him.

▶ Dig a little deeper:
   Read Ecclesiastes 11:9, 10

In Love Again?

KEY VERSE ▶

"Be kind and compassionate to one another, forgiving each other, just as in Christ God forgave you."

EPHESIANS 4:32

It was Mickey—Michelle Lewis—on the line. Kim was lying on her bed in her upstairs room, the telephone trapped between her ear and the pillow. She and Mickey were long-time, closest, best, most-trusted, dearest friends.

"Who is it this time?" Kim asked, a definite "ho-hum" in her voice. Mickey had begun the conversation by saying, "I'm in love again." To Kim it was getting boring, this series of short infatuations. During this school year alone there had been four—so far.

First it was Jim the computer nut, who invented a video game and named it after her. "Tricky Mickey," he called it. Big deal.

Then there was Karl the swimmer. Mickey was scared of water, so that didn't last long.

Then there was Corky the BMX bicycle racer.

Corky should have been the swimmer, Kim thought. He'd float easier. She smiled to herself. Anyway, Corky spent more time tuning up Mickey's ten-speed than he did talking to her.

The last one was Rory. He didn't do anything. He just was. Rory was suave, preppy. Kim didn't like him at all and couldn't understand why Mickey did. It didn't help that Rory barely noticed Kim, even when she and Mickey were standing together. Kim thought he was the supreme snob of the universe. That one ended when Mickey wore some weird combination of colors one day and Rory criticized her.

"Is that all he cares about?" Kim remembered her saying. "What colors I wear?"

"So, who is it this time?" Kim asked.

"You won't tell anyone?" Mickey cautioned.

"Am I your best friend?"

"Of course. You won't laugh?"

"Is it Justin Armstrong?" They both laughed. Justin Armstrong was a fourth grader that Kim and Mickey sometimes sat with on the Sunday school bus, squeezing three to a seat and teaching him Bible camp songs. They both adored him.

"Come on, Kim. This is serious."

"I thought it was serious the last eighteen times."

"You won't laugh?"

"I won't laugh."

"Promise?"

"I promise."

"Okay," said Mickey. "Remember, you promised."

"Okay, okay. Who is it?"

"It's Bobby Robbins.

"Robin Redbreast?" Kim snorted, slapping her hand over her mouth and trying not to laugh into the phone. Even best friends have trouble keeping promises sometimes. When she had recovered, she said, "I thought you used to call him a wimp."

"I guess I did. But I've changed my mind about him. I've been watching him—at school, and at church, too. He has strong ideas about stuff, even though he's so quiet."

"Does he have any strong ideas about you?"

"I don't think he's ever noticed me," Mickey said. "That's where you come in."

So Mickey and Kim entered into a conspiracy to entrap Bobby Robbins. He was in Kim's language arts class.

"You get to know him first," Mickey said to Kim, "and then you can start telling him all about me."

"You mean how you talk forever on the phone and never put the cap back on the toothpaste at sleepovers?"

"No. Tell him how smart I am and how wonderful and how beautiful."

"And he'll wonder why he hadn't noticed you before, right?"

"Right."

That's how it started. Kim and Bobby became friends. They worked on language arts assignments together, walked together in hallways, and somehow got on the same softball team in mixed gym.

Gradually they included Mickey in their activities, and the three of them became friends. That was exactly the way it was supposed to work. After that, Bobby and Mickey could become boyfriend and girlfriend.

The grand plan ended with the Valentine Day party at school. According to the plan, Bobby was supposed to invite Mickey. But he didn't. Bobby asked Kim!

"How could you?" Mickey said over the phone the night she heard. Kim hadn't told her, but news travels quickly around school. "How could you?" she repeated.

"I didn't," said Kim. "He did. What could I do about it?"

"You could have suggested he take me instead."

Kim thought about that a minute. She finally said, "I guess I was so surprised I just said yes without thinking." Which was, after all, partly true.

"Some friend you are."

"Bobby said you should go with us. We could double."

"You mean the three of us?"

"No, silly. With Paul Monson. He told Bobby he wants to ask you."

"Paul Monson? That character?"

"He's fun. He's Bobby's friend."

"I couldn't."

"That's one way to be with Bobby," Kim said, with an enticing kind of emphasis in her voice. "And who knows, maybe you'll get to like Paul."

"And what about you?" Mickey asked, speaking very slowly and seriously. "Do you like Bobby?"

"Of course I do. Didn't we agree two years ago that if one of us liked somebody, the other one would too?"

"I guess we did . . . although you never liked Rory."

"Well, forget Rory. Come on, Mick. We both like Bobby. We could both like Paul, too. We'll have fun."

"Okay. I guess so."

"I'll tell Bobby to tell Paul."

"Okay. But, Kim?"

"What?"

"You double-crossed me."

Kim smiled. She knew Mickey didn't mean it. Mickey knew she'd never hurt her on purpose. Not for Bobby or for Paul. Not for anyone. Friends like Mickey were hard to find.

▶ Dig a little deeper:

Read Ephesians 4:25—5:2

Fight-a-Teen

KEY VERSE ▶

"Don't let anyone look down on you because you are young, but set an example for the believers in speech, in life, in love, in faith and in purity."

I TIMOTHY 4:12

Scott had watched his parents losing their marriage for months, maybe years. He couldn't remember when the trouble had started. When he sat and thought about it now, he wondered if they had ever been suited for each other. He asked his mother once.

"Mom, what was it like for you and Dad when you were first married?"

"Oh, it was wonderful. We were young and in love and we were out to conquer the world together."

Scott noticed how his mother emphasized together. There was irony in her voice, and bitterness, too.

"What things did you plan?"

"Oh, at first your dad wanted to be an independent contractor. We sat up nights with pencils and scratch paper and worked out interest rates and depreciation and tax schedules. We talked for hours.

On Sundays after church we'd drive around town and look at sites we might buy to develop. We were out to conquer the world, I tell you."

"What happened?"

"Well, your dad took his job with Trilco, and the togetherness just sort of faded out. He became crew foreman, then job foreman, then project manager, then vice president."

"But it's not his company, right?"

"It's not our company. It would be partly yours by now too."

"I suppose it would. I never thought of that. And Tami's, too, if she were still around."

"Your father has been a good provider. He's very successful. I shouldn't complain."

"Maybe it would help if you didn't."

The minute Scott said it, he knew he had blown the conversation. His mother began weeping in that private silent way she had. Scott stood up from the kitchen chair, walked around the oak table, and put his arm around her shoulder. "I'm sorry," he said softly.

She reached up and patted his hand. "It's not your fault. I guess it's nobody's fault. The togetherness has just faded out of our marriage."

The phone rang. Scott answered, pointed at his mother to let her know it was for her, and then chatted politely with Mrs. Simms as his mother rinsed her face at the kitchen sink and, towel still in hand, took the call.

That was where the family stood just then. His father didn't talk much. His mother cried a lot.

They slept apart.

If they had never been suited for each other, Scott thought, what did that make him? A misfit? The product of a mismatch? He thought about a child born of a rape and how awesome a mismatch that was apt to be.

But his parents had loved each other once. Perhaps they still did, in spite of everything. He wanted to believe he was a product of their love, a living memory of their better times. He wondered if either of them looked at him sometimes and were sad that their love had faded. He was a mirror of their lost love.

Maybe they wish now they'd never had me, he thought, *or Tami, either.*

Then it struck him: *I, I myself, am what they still have in common. I am their hope. I am their gift of love to each other. God's gift to them. I was, and I still am. And Tami is too.*

Suddenly he felt powerful. He felt he had leverage, even if he didn't know quite how to use it.

He wished there were a group he could join to talk things over with other kids, and maybe some adults— how to handle his parents, how to use his love leverage to do whatever he could, how to be a weld and not a wedge.

There's Alanon and Alateen, he thought. Why not something for kids of parents in trouble? Fightanon or Bickerateen. The names were stupid, but the idea wasn't funny. Not a bit ridiculous.

Scott decided to walk over to the church and see if Pastor Ames was there. He could just hedge into a conversation, maybe, casually mentioning his parents' difficulties, and see if the pastor thought it would be okay to start a Fight-a-Teen group.

It would be a beginning. At their first meeting, though, they'd have to come up with something less stupid for a name.

▶ Dig a little deeper:

Read Philippians 4:4-7

Jingle Jorgenson, Adopted

KEY VERSE ▶

*"The Spirit himself testifies
with our spirit that we are
God's children."*

ROMANS 8:16

"Did you hear me, Pepper?" Jingle whispered. "I'm adopted." We were alone in the deserted gymnasium. In the halls, kids shouted and laughed as they headed out of school for the weekend.

"What do you mean?" I asked.

"Adopted. You know the word. Orphanage. Foundling." She began to sob. "The baby left on the church door in a basket. The whole bit."

"Come on, Jingle. Don't get dramatic. Who says you're adopted?"

"My parents. My mom. The woman I live with who isn't my mom. I don't even know what to call her now. She told me last night."

"Why didn't you tell me this morning?"

Jingle just shrugged.

"And why didn't they tell you before?"

"I don't know."

"If you aren't Jingle Jorgenson, who are you?"

"That's the scary part. I don't know." She sucked in a sob.

"Where were you born?"

"I don't know that, either. Maybe I'm from Bethlehem."

"Bethlehem? Come on, Jingle. In a stable? Your mother was a carpenter? Your father a virgin?" I was hoping it was all a joke.

"Bethlehem, Pennsylvania," she said. "My parents lived there when I was a baby. You know that." She sounded almost angry that I had forgotten.

"Yeah, I guess I did. How old were you when they got you? Did you ask your mom any questions?"

"I was a baby."

"How about Chip? Is he adopted too?"

"Yup."

"Are you brother and sister—I mean really?"

"Nope."

"Does he know he's adopted?"

"He's known for a long time, I guess."

"Then *he* should have told you."

"I wish he had." My best friend, Jingle Jorgenson, was devastated. She was really crying now. She sagged down on a bleacher bench. I took two steps over and sat down beside her. The gym was empty. Her sobs echoed into that emptiness. I'll bet she felt at least that empty inside.

"I don't know who I am anymore," Jingle sobbed.

"You're who you always were."

"But I'm not, don't you see?" She blew her nose

on a paper napkin she had pulled from her jeans pocket. "I used to look at my mom—Mrs. Jorgenson, I guess I should call her now—and see myself when I got older. Now all I see is a stranger."

"She's not a stranger. She's still your mother."

"But I have a real mother out there somewhere— and a real father, too. That's what I'm going to be like. That's my real pattern." She began to sob again.

I was near crying myself. I had my right arm around Jingle's shoulders, and with my left thumb was directing tears off her cheeks so they wouldn't drip in her lap. *Cruel,* I thought.

The janitor came into the gym and saw us. "I'm locking up now," he said. We got up and walked arm in arm toward the big double doors.

"You okay?" he asked Jingle, seeing she had been crying. Jingle nodded.

"I'll take care of her, thanks, Mr. Wells," I said as we walked by. *He's a nice man. Wish he were a teacher.* To Jingle I said, "Want to go to your locker?"

"No."

"It's Friday. You need books and stuff. Come on."

"Okay," she said, not bothering to resist.

We went to Jingle's locker. I watched as she took out several spiral notebooks and two textbooks. She moved like a zombie.

"That enough stuff?" I asked.

"Who cares?"

"I care. You'll live through this, Jingle. Besides, I want us to graduate in the same class." I tried a small smile. No response.

"I s'pose," she mumbled.

"Walk me to my locker, then I'll walk you home."

"Where is my home, Pepper?"

That's when I started to cry. "Where your home has always been," I finally managed to say.

"It doesn't seem like my home anymore."

"We're going there, though." I took her arm and walked her to my locker, took out a book bag, stuffed in a few things, slammed the door, spun the combination lock decisively, and said, "Let's go."

We walked in silence. I held Jingle's arm, directing her along the sidewalk and across the streets as if she were blind. As we walked, my mind flashed back to the day we met. It was in the grocery store. Our mothers had met first at church, so they introduced us.

"This is Jeanine Jorgenson," Mom said to me, beaming. "She's just moved here from Ohio."

"We call her 'Jingle,' " her mother said.

"And we call her 'Pepper,' " my mother said, pointing to me.

That was our introduction. We were friends in two days, best friends in two weeks. Jingle and Pepper, inseparable. That was two years ago. We have suffered through a lot together—like last year, when our neighborhood was redistricted, and Jingle and I began busing to the other high school across town. And the two months last summer when Mom and Dad were fighting all the time and Dad moved out and then moved back in again. Jingle was so good about that. These things and more. I was sure we could get Jingle through this crisis as well.

As we neared Jingle's house, she said, "I'm not sure I want to go there."

"It's your home, Crazy."

"It was."

"It still is. Besides, if you don't go in now, it will be harder tonight, and harder yet tomorrow. Do it now."

"Why did they wait so long?" she asked, her foot hovering over the first of her front steps.

"I don't know. They didn't do it to be cruel, that's for sure." I heard myself saying it, but I only half believed it. "Come on. I'll go in with you."

Mrs. Jorgenson came out of the kitchen the minute she heard the front door. She was still in her white uniform. She probably had come home from work early—and I guessed Jingle was the reason.

"I'm so glad you're home," Mrs. J. said. "I called the school and no one was around."

"She's been with me," I said.

"I'm so sorry about this morning, Jingle. She told you?" Mrs. J. asked, turning to me.

"Yes," I said, noncommittally. I wanted to hear her side of it. But at that moment I felt a lot more sympathetic toward Jingle than toward her mom.

"I knew it was wrong. I've known for years. But the longer you put off something like that, the harder it gets."

"Who are my real parents?" Jingle asked her mother.

"We don't know that much. We got you through an agency of our church in Bethlehem. Chip, too.

Your mother was a young girl. Probably about your age."

"And my father?"

"Her boyfriend. A high school boy. That's all they told us, except that she came from a home and family rather like ours is right now."

"Why didn't you have your own children?" Jingle asked. Her eyes were flashing, accusing, as if her mom and dad had somehow chosen to be childless.

"We couldn't have our own children, Jingle. After a few years we knew we never would. Then we got you and Chip, and after that it didn't seem to matter. You were ours. Our very own. We love you both so much. Your dad was satisfied with that, and so was I."

"My dad is somewhere in Pennsylvania."

"Come on, Jingle," I said. "Be fair." I was on Mrs. J's side now. "That's your mom." I pointed. "What other family have you ever had?"

"I have another family. Somewhere." There was an awkward silence.

"They open court records a lot these days," her mother said at last. "Some adopted children find their biological parents. Do you want that?"

"I don't know. I need to get used to being adopted first, I guess."

"We love you," Mrs. J. said softly, holding out her arms in an invitation.

As Jingle walked hesitantly into her mother's arms, she began to cry again. It was a different cry this time. Not a hurt cry but a lonely cry, a cry that seemed to ask why the world had to be this way, why Jingle once had a mother who couldn't keep her, and now had another father and mother who wanted her so very much, and loved her and loved her brother and loved each other. That cry finally got around to making me ask myself why my very own parents don't even know if they love each other or want to live together anymore. That made me want to cry.

Mrs. J. must have seen that look on my face. She turned to me, and then, as if someone had whispered to both of them at once, both she and Jingle unclasped their arms and opened them to me, like the open arms of Jesus. I slowly walked in alongside of Jingle, into that love machine that was her adopted mother. A three-way hug. I wondered how Jingle's other mother would feel if she could see it: her daughter, almost grown up, being hugged by a mother and a friend who loved her. Would she be pleased that Jingle, her mistake, her accident, was so loved and cared for?

I turned and looked at the side of Jingle's face. She was beautiful. Even crying she was beautiful. She's one of the prettiest girls in our school. Her mother was probably that way, too—pretty, attractive, the kind older boys hang around. I wondered if Jingle's other mother had ever experienced anywhere near the love Jingle has. I wondered if, fifteen years ago, Jingle's young mom had needed love very badly and, mistaking sex for love, wrapped herself around that high school boy and got Jingle started inside herself.

I wished that boy could be here now, watching this. Are there ever going to be some guys who care about what happens to girls? Will they ever quit being so selfish that they can't see the Jingles nine months—or for that matter, fifteen years—down the line?

Jingle was one of the lucky ones, I guess. It's different for a lot of unwanted babies. They stay with their little-girl moms or they go to live with their grandmas, and the cycle goes on and on. Yeah, I guess Jingle was lucky. Mr. and Mrs. Jorgenson may have goofed in not telling her sooner, but at least they love her—and that's a lot.

"You two going to be okay?" I asked.

"Yes, Pepper, I think so," Mrs. J. said. "Thanks so much for being Jingle's very, very good friend."

I started to cry again.

When we all had calmed down, I stepped away. As I was walking toward the door, I said, "Call me tonight, Jingle, okay?"

"Okay, Pep," she responded with our private joke, "I'll give you a jingle."

▶ Dig a little deeper:

Read Romans 8:15-17, 35-39

The Basketball

KEY VERSE ▶

"If you, then, though you are evil, know how to give good gifts to your children, how much more will your Father in heaven give good gifts to those who ask him!"

MATTHEW 7:11

Tim had more than an average hard time setting up the basketball court in his driveway. He had no father to help—and his mother was about as mechanical as a chess champion.

They got through it, though. Tim, his mother, and his friend Luke. Lamb Chop watched the whole operation. She barked, teased, and got in the way as only a mongrel poodle could. Tim and Luke even put her down in the post hole and took a picture before they set the backboard stand in place. Her white curls got a bit dirty, but she didn't mind.

The basketball court was a superb cooperative venture. His mother had paid for the post and the plywood. Luke had dipped into his savings to buy the hoop and net. Tim did most of the dirty work. And of course Lamb Chop encouraged them at every stage. But they had no ball.

They started to play with a plastic beach ball before the paint was even dry. It was some fun, to be sure, but Tim was already on his way to playing varsity basketball in the next few years. What good was a wimpy ball you had to aim way to the side in a cross-wind—and throw overhand like a baseball from the deep back court? His timing would be way off if he didn't get a real ball.

"I'll buy a basketball on time payments, Tim announced to Luke after church on Sunday.

"Who'll sell you one that way?"

"Mr. Sherwin. In his hardware store."

"Rotsa ruck," said Luke.

But Mr. Sherwin did set up a time payment plan for Tim.

First thing Monday morning, Tim bought their very best official size and weight basketball—and signed a paper agreeing to pay a dollar a week out of his allowance.

All that first delightful afternoon they played, using Lamb Chop as their opposition. They dribbled around her, passed over her, faked the ball toward her nose and then shot, completely ignoring her barking insistence that they were hogging the ball.

"Let's take a break," said Luke, sinking down to his knees, panting in absolute exhaustion.

Tim agreed. "How about some milk and peanut butter toast?"

Tim set the ball in the middle of the cement slab and they went in. A quart of milk and eleven slices of toast later they ran back outside, ready for the second half.

"Where's the ball?" Luke asked.

"I left it right here."

They scouted around. Something else was missing.

"Where's Lamb Chop?" Luke asked.

Then they heard a bark down toward the end of the driveway. Tim gasped, "Oh, no."

She was nuzzling the ball along the driveway toward the street. They watched as, almost in slow motion, Lamb Chop nosed the ball into the air one last time, like a trained water show seal. It bounced twice, then rolled the remaining ten yards down the driveway and out onto the pavement where the dual rear wheels of a passing semitrailer truck promptly flattened it. The explosion sounded like a gunshot. Lamb Chop slunk back alongside of them with her tail between her legs.

The bang sounded to Tim like the final gun in a losing game, a humiliating losing game, an eighty-five to eighteen loss. His dream of varsity basketball went poof, and his twenty-nine-dollar debt suddenly loomed large. He hauled back and kicked Lamb Chop on the flanks. Hard.

Instantly he was sorry, but it was too late. The poodle scooted under the porch deck, her hiding place of last resort. Tim could still hear the semi, changing gears up the hill toward town.

Tim and Luke walked back with the flattened ball, threw it by the back door, and slumped onto the back step. There they sat, chins on hands, elbows on knees, for twenty minutes or more. Neither of them said a word. Tim thought, toward the last, that he heard the sound of a semi idling out front, but decided it was just his anger bubbling away inside him like a diesel engine.

His mother opened the back door, stepped out,

picked up the flat ball, and disappeared again into the kitchen. Several minutes later she reappeared on the deck with money in her hand.

"The truck driver came back," she said, "and paid for the ball. He said they have a slush fund in the office to pay little claims. Keeps insurance rates down and goodwill up."

Tim looked at the money. A twenty and a ten. His mother, smiling, urged it toward him. But he was standing there wishing he hadn't kicked Lamb Chop. How could he have kicked their friendship away so easily, so cheaply? Just twenty-nine dollars. He wouldn't take a million for Lamb Chop.

As he reached out his hand for the money, Tim felt a familiar nuzzle on his ankle. He turned, knelt, handed the green bills to Luke, and swept Lamb Chop up into his arms.

He thought of his mother and of Luke and of the truck driver and of Lamb Chop and of God.

"There is love in the world," Tim whispered to himself. Aloud he shouted to Luke, "Let's go down to Sherwin's and get a new ball."

He set Lamb Chop down, then he and Luke vaulted onto their bikes in perfect synchrony. Luke had the bills clamped in his teeth. Lamb Chop trailed them at a dead run to the end of the driveway, her tail drawing corkscrew circles in the summer air.

▶ Dig a little deeper:

Matthew 7:7-12

How Did It Feel?

KEY VERSE ▶

" '. . . Neither do I condemn
you,' Jesus declared. 'Go now
and leave your life of sin.' "

JOHN 8:11

"How did it feel? Did it feel good?"
   "Sure it did."
   "Then why did you quit?"
   "My life was changed."
   "Changed how?"
   "I became a Christian."
   "Was quitting like that hard?"
   "Not very. It was harder for him, I think."
   "But what did it feel like? I mean really?"
   "I don't think we should talk about that."
   It bothered Carmen, those questions. They popped
up whenever she went along to church groups with
Margie, her youth director friend, to give talks about
teen sexuality. Margie did most of the talking at these
events; Carmen went along as a kind of walking case
history. She would tell about her two-year relationship
with John, how it started and how it stopped and how

it had affected her, and how she felt about it now. Her part of the program was a kind of testimonial.

Then afterward, they'd be sitting around in small groups drinking soda and eating popcorn and some girl would ask, "How does it feel?" Not "How do you feel about it," but "How does it feel?" The big IT. She knew what they wanted to hear, and she was always glad someone would feel free enough to ask her, but she didn't want to tell them. She was the same age as most of the kids, even younger than some of them, but in some ways she felt so much older.

Driving home one night, Carmen asked Margie about it.

They had been driving along in silence for ten minutes or more, the tires sizzling along on the wet pavement. They were often silent after these meetings; they were usually pretty well talked out and silence felt good. But tonight Carmen wanted to talk.

"I feel guilty," she began, "when kids ask me how it feels."

"You mean sex?"

"Yes."

"Why guilty?"

"I mean, what kind of witness is it if I say it feels good?"

"Does it feel good?"

"You don't know?"

"No."

"But you're engaged."

"I expect a lot of people, and especially religious people, are engaged and don't have sex."

"And I expect a lot of them do."

"It depends for some of us on whether we see it as a religious issue. Obviously, I do. That's why I go out, or we go out, and do these little sexy seminars."

Carmen smiled. That's what she and Margie privately called their program.

"You were talking about your witness. . . ." Margie said.

"And you were asking me how it felt," Carmen answered.

"Yes."

"That's the problem, see. Everyone who hasn't tried it wants to know how it feels."

"Of course we do."

"But how can I tell that part? Would God want me to go on like an X-rated movie?"

"No, I don't think God would want that. But you could be honest about it, maybe."

"But it felt good."

"So what's wrong with that? If it didn't, I expect we wouldn't have to go out all the time and talk to kids about it."

"But it doesn't feel good at first."

"You have to tell that part too."

"That's for sure. If girls could know how it feels the first time, and how they'd likely feel about themselves afterward, they probably wouldn't."

"That's what we're after, isn't it?"

"But if I tell about 'at first,' I'm going to have to tell about 'after a while.' "

"How does it feel after a while?"

"After a while it starts to feel good. A total feeling, a feeling of being completely loved, and of doing something so special for him, something he enjoys so much."

"A lot of people I've talked to who have intercourse before marriage," Margie said, "say they wish they had waited. They say it's so much better after marriage, with total commitment and trust, and with the fear and secrecy and the sneakiness all gone."

"I expect it would be better that way," Carmen said quietly. Her throat choked up. She wondered if she would ever find some Christian young man who would accept her as she was now, forgive her for what she had been, and be willing to start out fresh and new together. Margie assured her she would find someone, that God probably had that someone already picked out.

Carmen wished she could be that sure. There were times when she felt so used, especially when she talked to kids her own age who seemed so innocent, so untouched. It made her sad inside.

Then she'd think of Jesus and what innocence really meant. Forgiveness had washed over her last summer like a warm shower. Whenever she needed to get out of a blue mood, or to feel better about herself, she would think back to that campfire and that wonderful woman pastor who talked, and how she had gone forward, and how hands were laid on her and prayers were said, and how, after everyone else had hit the bunks, she and that woman had taken a canoe and paddled in the moonlight all the way around the calm lake. They talked, Carmen confessed, and when they got back to the camp dock almost at dawn, she remembered that wonderful woman saying:

"I know you don't need another baptizing, but maybe a kind of washing would seal this night in our memories."

They had walked into the water, waist deep, clothes and all. The woman took water in her cupped hand and poured it over Carmen's forehead and prayed. Carmen was sure she looked a lot like King David being anointed. Or maybe like Jesus and John the Baptist in the Jordan River.

Anyway, it felt good, oh, it felt so good to be forgiven. She felt like a queen. And it had lasted. It was still there. Forgiveness. The love of Jesus. That feeling lasted at home the following week. It lasted through a very trying month or so with John. He never did understand what Carmen had been through. They broke up. But the forgiveness and the other love lasted. Carmen knew afterward that their love, hers and John's, had been too physical, too much based on sex.

As they whooshed along in the car, Carmen still felt washed, and forgiven, and restored. Sitting there with Margie, she still felt good about who she was, and who she was becoming. The only time she ever felt bad about who she used to be was when they'd ask, "How did it feel?" Carmen wondered if that would ever change.

▶ Dig a little deeper: John 8:2-11

Vocational Motivation

KEY VERSE ▶

"Trust in the Lord with all your heart and lean not on your own understanding; in all your ways acknowledge him, and he will make your paths straight."

PROVERBS 3:5, 6

"I don't have a clue. Not a whisper of an idea," Paul said.

"Well, it's not the end of the world," Scott said. "Not everyone knows in grade school what he wants to do with the rest of his life."

"But I'm supposed to start college next fall, and I won't have a major, or even an interest. Like Mr. Holden says, I don't have any . . . Vocational Motivation." They said it in unison and laughed.

Their English teacher's phrase had become a byword among the senior class. You'd go down the hall and see someone slumped against a locker looking tired, and two or three friends walking by would pipe up in unison, "What's the matter? Don't you have any . . . Vocational Motivation?"

But Paul really didn't have any. How could he hope for a home, a family, a good life if he didn't have any direction, any goals? Maybe he ought to talk to Mr. Holden. The kids laughed at Mr. Holden's phrase, but they knew he was one teacher who really cared about them.

"Hi, Paul. What you up to?" Mr. Holden said. He was rearranging his room after the last class.

"I'm up to nothing. That's why I'm here."

"What do you mean?"

"My future. It seems so hopeless."

"You've gotta be kidding."

"I wish I were."

"But look at you. You get decent grades. You come from a solid, two-parent home; you've held down a part-time job for . . . how long have you worked at Arnie's?"

"Three years."

"See?"

"But everyone else is planning to be a doctor or a lawyer or a preacher or a farmer. I'm not planning anything."

"So, because you're not planning anything, you think you can't do anything?"

"Right."

"Wrong." Mr. Holden smiled. "Listen, Paul. You're one of the top ten kids I've had in my classes this year. You don't always get the best grades, but I mean all around. You discuss things well, and you listen. And your essays are sometimes so wrong that they're right."

"What does that mean?"

"I mean you think an essay question so far beyond

a high school textbook level that you sometimes get into essences."

"Essences? Isn't that smells? You saying my essays stink?" They both laughed.

"When I'm reading a set of essay answers and yours comes up early, I bury it near the bottom of the pile . . . ."

"Because it stinks." Neither of them laughed this time.

"No. I put it near the end so that when I'm tired and bored with the standard answers, I can be perked up with something unusual. Sometimes you're way off the subject, but you're always deep. You may be a philosopher."

"What's that?"

"In Greek the word means 'lover of wisdom.' Philosophy is something you can study in college and in graduate school. It's a way of thinking, of finding things out."

"What do philosophers do?"

"Well, some of them change the world—like Karl Marx or Charles Darwin or Sigmund Freud—or Saint Paul in the Bible."

"And the rest of them? The rest of us?" He smiled.

"They teach, mostly. And write books."

"And you think I'm a philosopher?"

"You might be. Or a theologian. Theologians are kind of like philosophers who think about God. If I were you I'd register for introductory philosophy my first semester in college—and maybe religion."

• • •

They talked for another ten minutes or so, and then Paul headed out. Leaving school, he ran into Scott, who had his mountain bike upside down and was messing with the derailleur.

"There," Scott pronounced, turning it right side up. "So, how's my hopeless friend?"

"Better," said Paul. "I've discovered I'm a philosopher."

"A what?"

"A philosopher."

"Isn't that somebody from Philadelphia?" Scott said with a grin.

"Right," Paul agreed, "with a lot of . . . Vocational Motivation!"

▶ Dig a little deeper:

Read Proverbs 3:1-18

A World without Harper

KEY VERSE ▶

*"There will be no more death
or mourning or crying or
pain, for the old order of
things has passed away."*

REVELATION 21:4

Kristy sat on her bed, staring at one of Harper's posters. Her mother called up the stairs: "That was Lauren. She'll pick you up in ten minutes."

There was an unusual gentleness in her voice, Kristy noticed. It was different from her mother's usual morning voice: "You have to get up now," or her after-supper voice: "You'll be late for choir."

Maybe she understands what I'm going through, Kristy thought. *No, she couldn't. When your best friend commits suicide, who understands how you feel?*

When Lauren drove up in her red Subaru—Super Boo, they called it—Kristy was ready. They were both dressed like they were heading for yuppie job interviews: conservative combinations of black, gray, and white. Heels. Clutch purses in hand. Neither of them had put on any eye makeup.

There would be more crying at church.

They sat silently in the car a minute before starting out, the engine throbbing quietly, a surprisingly soothing sound.

"Why did she do it?" Lauren asked, as she pulled away from the curb.

"I don't know. I still can't believe it."

"She didn't even leave a note."

They'd been over all this a hundred times in the last three days, but they had to talk about it again.

"Do you think it was because they were moving?" asked Kristy.

"Lots of people move."

"Lots of kids commit suicide, too. Hundreds. There have to be reasons."

"Only God understands," Lauren said.

"What does God think about it, do you suppose? I mean, does Harper get in or not?" Kristy really wanted to know.

"She was so stainless steel before this. I would have called her one of the most religious kids in our class," Lauren said.

"I know." Kristy remembered when she and Harper were at the youth convention and she and Harper and Lauren went to church camp together and how their group always went to Taco Bell after church choir practice and ate tacos by the dozen.

Suddenly she began to cry again. She didn't work up to it as she had done at home. Here in Super Boo with Lauren, in a moment's time, she was weeping uncontrollably. Lauren pulled the car over to the side of the road, then leaned across the gearshift console and put her arm around Kristy's shoulder.

"Why did she do this to us?" Kristy sobbed.

"She did it to herself."

"No, she did it to us. To her folks. To our church. Our teachers. Everybody."

"At least she won't have to move," Lauren said softly. "Now she'll be in this town forever.

"Yeah. Oaklawn Cemetery. Big deal."

Kristy and Lauren silently shared the irony of it. In another context they might have laughed. It was Harper's sick joke on them, and they knew it. But there was nothing funny about it.

"She wouldn't have had to move." Kristy tried hard to talk normally. "She could have lived at our place and graduated with our class. We talked about it."

"Moving wasn't the only reason."

"She gave me her posters last week," Kristy said.

"Did she? I got her Bill Cosby stuff."

"You mean the tapes—and the autographed program?"

"All of it. We should have known when she started giving stuff away." Lauren wiggled back into the bucket seat and pulled the car away from the curb.

"She said it was because they were moving."

"Would you give your tape collection away if you moved?"

"No," Kristy said emphatically. "You're right; we should have known." Then she added, "She really did it to us." There was anger in her voice now, along with the sadness. "If I could bring her back, I'd chew her out but good."

"But we can't," Lauren said. "That's the worst thing about it. They kick you in the face and they're gone."

"How could she?" Kristy's question was painfully plaintive.

"I guess she couldn't help it." Lauren was trying to be the wise and strong one.

"Why didn't she let us know? Why wouldn't she let us help her?"

"Did she ever?" Lauren mused on it for a moment, then went on. "Did Harper ever ask anyone for anything?"

"No, I guess not. She always had to get things right—by herself."

"She sure did this by herself," Lauren said after a long pause.

"Damn," Kristy whispered.

"That's what I'm worried about."

"Me, too," Kristy said. "God help her."

"Lord save her," Lauren added.

"Amen," Kristy whispered.

There was no more to be said. Kristy thought of Harper's lonely and desperate act and how many people it had hurt. Quietly she vowed that she would never hurt anyone like that. Ever.

At the church parking lot she got out of the car and walked hand in hand with Lauren into the church, still thinking and praying privately, silently. Sadly, reluctantly she moved into the building . . . and into a new world, a more sober and less happy world . . . a world without her friend Harper.

▶ Dig a little deeper: Revelation 21:1-6

The Replacement

KEY VERSE ▶

". . . He is not the God of the
dead but of the living."

MATTHEW 22:32

"You can't love him."

"Of course I can. And I do."

"But you loved my dad."

"Yes, I did. I still do. But he's been dead for three years."

"That's not so long to remember."

"I do remember him. And I cherish those memories. I just don't want to be alone anymore."

"You're not alone. You have me. And Heather. And Grandma and Grandpa, too."

"It's not the same. I can't expect you to understand that at your age. But it's just not the same."

"I don't want another father. Heather doesn't either. She said so."

"No one will ever replace your father for you and Heather. For me either, I guess. But sometimes we

50

have to start over. Sometimes we have to try again."

"Maybe this time it won't work out. Then what?"

"It will work out between Carl and me. It's already working out. What I'm praying for is that Carl will work out for you and Heather as well."

"Don't mention praying to me. If praying made things work out, Dad would still be here."

"I prayed for your father too. Our whole church did. God knows we all prayed. God didn't answer my prayer, either. Or at least not in the way I expected. I never wanted to be a widow. I never wanted to remarry. But that seems best to me now. And that's what I plan to do."

"That's what we don't want you to do. It's like hitting Dad when he can't fight back."

"It's not hitting him, honey. He's gone. He's with God. Nothing can hurt him now."

"But it can hurt me. And Heather."

"Don't I know that? I'm not trying to hurt either of you. I keep telling myself that I'm doing this partly for you kids, so you can have a father."

"We had a father already."

"Had is exactly right. What I mean is a real, live father. Someone you can learn from. Someone you can do things with. What they call a role model."

"You don't have to marry Carl for him to be a role model."

"Marrying him makes it seem all the more right somehow. Marrying him gives him the right to be your father."

"Or try to be."

"Won't you let him?"

"I don't know him yet."

"He's a good man. He's not trying to kidnap you, or take away any of the love you have for your own father."

"I s'pose not. But it isn't the same."

"It will never be the same. The minute your father took his last breath everything changed."

"I know. Why did God do this to us?"

"It's okay to cry, honey. Men cry. Your father did. Come here. God didn't do this to us. It just happened. God doesn't kill fathers—or husbands, either."

"God let Dad die."

"Sure he did. He let His own Son die too. God knows how we feel."

"Not likely."

"I think he does know. Really."

"But Jesus came back to life. My dad isn't going to do that."

"I know. That 's the hard part. But now isn't the only time. There's forever. Your father is waiting for you there."

"He's waiting for you, too. What's he going to say when you show up with another husband?"

"That's better. That's my boy. It's better when you're smiling."

"I don't feel like smiling."

"But you will. There'll be a lot of happy times. Carl isn't exactly like your father. But he's a good man. And I love him. It's hard for me to imagine you disliking someone I love—for very long anyway."

"It's not the same for me."

"I know. But you'll learn. Will you try?"

"I don't know."

"Please?"

"I can't speak for Heather."

"If you try, so will Heather. You know how she trusts you. Will you? Please?"

"Well . . ."

"For me?"

"Well . . ."

"And for God?"

"For God?"

"The God who knows how you feel? Who let His Son die?"

"I s'pose."

"Good. Want some lunch?"

▶ Dig a little deeper:

Read I Corinthians 15:42-57

Churchgoing

KEY VERSE ▶

"... There will be more rejoicing in heaven over one sinner who repents than over ninety-nine righteous persons who do not need to repent."

LUKE 15:7

It was Palm Sunday. Maria wouldn't have known that, but the bulletin board outside the church said so. "Back to the Big city" was the title of the day's sermon. Ha. The sermon Maria needed to hear was "Back to the Small Town." She stood outside the church for a long time, debating whether she should go in. She recalled how long it had been since she had last been to church—over two years and 500 miles from where she now stood. She had not gone to church since that last Sunday at home with her mother. It wasn't a pleasant memory.

"Didn't Mrs. Morel look like a fashion plate today?" her mother said as they walked home from the service.

"She always does. You would too, if you had her money."

54

"I wouldn't know what to do with her money."

"I would. I'd quit school and blow this wimpy town and this wimpy church and its wimpy people."

Maria's mother said nothing. She just walked into the house, went to the hall closet, and hung her coat in silence. She was hurt, Maria knew, but Maria couldn't have kept from saying it if she had tried—and she wasn't sorry.

Home had become stifling, and so had school, and so had her life. Stifling. Boring. She was ready to explode. Maybe, just maybe, if she left town, she wouldn't have to explode.

She went to her desk to find her savings passbook. There was almost enough in her account to get her to Denver and get her settled, especially if Bud helped. Bud had said again and again that he would take her in if she came to Denver.

Maria had quit school. She'd gone to Denver. And Bud had taken her in: into his apartment, into his bed, into the Denver drug scene. Her savings were gone in several months. Bud was gone in less than a year. But the scars remained. She had been burned—and had burned all her bridges. Home was 500 miles away. It might as well be 500 light years.

But just one ordinary year later, things seemed much better. Maria scrolled the whole memory through her mind as she stood outside the church: her solitary life at the YWCA, the counseling, her move into a one-room flat, finding the new job—a job that wasn't half bad. On good days she actually enjoyed going to work.

But there was a gnawing inside that wouldn't go away. Not having finished school gnawed. The guarded and cool trickle of letters she and her mother exchanged gnawed. And a vague sense of guilt or unforgiven sin gnawed.

So Maria stood hesitantly, tentatively in front of the old church and thought about the Palm Sunday story as she remembered it. The gist of it, she recalled, was that everyone welcomed Jesus into town with a big ticker tape parade; then in less than a week they turned on Him and nailed Him to a tree.

Sometimes you can't tell who your friends are, she said to herself. *Jesus' friends turned against him in a few days. It took Bud half a year, but the result was the same. I should have known better,* she thought.

Maria stood there and studied the front of the church for a few minutes more, then said to herself, *Why not?*

She walked into the big church, dark with oak, the inside space multicolored by light that filtered through the stained glass. Spring hadn't gotten inside yet; it smelled like the musty stub of a long winter. She sat down in a back pew and looked at her watch.

It was good to be in a church again. It was good to be in God's space. She remembered a poem she had once read called "Churchgoing." The person in the poem rode a bicycle. She remembered an image of a cemetery and the man saying something like, "It's a place for serious thought."

A church is that way, she told herself. *A place for serious thought.* She thought of her religious mother and her religious upbringing and of how important religion had been to her back in junior high. She had even wanted to be a nun until her mother said they didn't have nuns in their church.

Her dream of a convent was soon gone—but not her dream of God. It lurked in her soul like an egg about to hatch. Should she try to find her faith again? Could she?

There was a tap on her shoulder, and Maria turned to meet the smile of a woman. She was somewhat older than Maria's mother, but not unlike her mother in dress and movement and features.

"Are you new in town?" the lady asked.

"Yes. Yes, I am." Maria said, lying and yet not lying.

Suddenly Denver did seem new to her. There were other sides to Denver, sides she hadn't seen yet. Bud's seamy side of town wasn't the only Denver. This nice lady lived in Denver too—and so did her family and her friends and a lot of other good people like her mom.

"Yes," Maria repeated. "I'm new. I have a new job."

Just then the big old organ began a variation on "Just As I Am." Maria was not only enveloped in the music, she was swept up into the arms of God.

She vowed at that moment that she would look into finishing high school at night, and that right after the service she would write her mother and tell her so. Better yet, she would call. Even better: before calling, she would check the bus schedule for Thursday. She had Good Friday and Monday off. She could spend Easter with her mother. They could celebrate both resurrections.

Maria turned as the organist introduced "Lead On, O King Eternal," and whispered to the lady, "Thank you." Then, facing the marble altar with the book and the candles on it, she wept silently, motionlessly—and tried to remember how long it had been since her cheeks had been baptized in tears.

▶ Dig a little deeper:

Read Luke 15:1-10

Seeing a Movie with Ann

KEY VERSE ▶

" . . . The Lord does not look
at the things man looks at.
Man looks at the outward
appearance, but the Lord
looks at the heart."

I SAMUEL 16:7

"Hey, Mom?" There was a large question mark in Jay's voice, a tone that usually meant something heavy was coming—a religious or philosophical or social action question was about to be raised.

"Yes?" his mother said, looking up from her typewriter. She seemed to be bracing herself for the worst.

"Do I dare ask Ann Wright to a movie?"

"What's wrong with Ann Wright? Is she a grandmother or what?"

"Oh, Mom."

"Well, who is Ann Wright?"

"She's the one who stays with the Tracys and goes to our school."

"Oh. That's her name. Ann Wright. She's very pretty. No. She's more than pretty, she's utterly beautiful. Does she ever go out on dates?"

59

"Not that I know of."

"Maybe a movie isn't the best choice."

"But I can't think of anything else that she and I could do in this town."

"Does she roller-skate or anything?"

"I don't know. She's out for the swim team—but who takes a girl swimming on a first date? I mean, do I go up to her and say, 'Hi, Ann. How about us going swimming together'?"

"How well do you know her?"

"Pretty well, I guess. About as well as any of the guys."

"Then why don't you just ask her? Let her decide. Just say"—his mom assumed a gruff voice—"Ann? How would you feel about going to a movie with me?"

Jay laughed out loud. "I'll try it," he said, picking up the phone.

"Ann. Hi. This is Jay. How would you feel about going to a movie with me tomorrow night?" Jay felt only a little strange about using his mother's exact words.

"Oh, Jay, that would be just great."

"You're sure? About a movie, I mean?"

"Really, Jay. I love movies. I just don't get to go that often."

They talked for a few minutes. "I'll pick you up about six-thirty, okay?" Jay asked.

"Sure. How are we going to get there?"

"Do you mind walking?"

"No. I love to walk. I just asked so I'd know what

to wear."

"Good. I'll see you at six-thirty then."

"Thanks, Jay."

Thanks, Jay. The sound of her mellow voice echoed in his mind. Jay walked upstairs to his room, mumbling to himself, "How can the guys in our school be so stupid as not to ask her out? She's a little scary, I suppose. But she is going out with me. Maybe that will get some of the other guys started. Maybe I don't want to get the other guys started. Maybe I'll want to keep her for myself. We'll see."

Jay arrived at the Tracy house at six-thirty sharp.

"Ann will be down in a minute, Jay," said Mrs. Tracy. "It's nice that you two are going to a film. Ann doesn't get to do that very often."

Ann appeared at the top of the stairs just then. She had on jeans, Adidas, and a short-sleeved blouse, just what all the girls wore. Her brown hair was soft and fluffy, and she wore dark glasses.

"She *is* beautiful," Jay said to himself. "Just like Mom says. She looks like a movie star."

"Well, say something, Jay," Ann said from the top of the stairs.

"You look real nice."

"Thanks." Ann followed that compliment as if it were a golden thread tying them together. Down the stairs she came and stood at Jay's elbow, slipping her hand inside of his forearm.

"Well, Aunt Jean, we're on our way," Ann said.

"Have fun, you two."

"We won't be late," Jay said. "We may stop at Mork's Café after the show, if that's okay."

"How about if I start worrying about eleven or eleven-thirty?"

"That would be great," Jay said as they walked out. "She's nice," he said to Ann when they were out on the sidewalk. "I didn't know she was your aunt."

"She's my most favorite aunt. What have you heard about the show?"

"Bill and Beth saw it yesterday," Jay told her. "Bill said it was pretty good. . . ."

They walked and talked, crossing the streets with some care but practically flying in between.

"I love to walk fast," she said.

"You're good at it," Jay said squeezing her hand against his ribs.

The film started slowly. Jay kept whispering a kind of play by play in Ann's ear. From behind it didn't look like a first date. Their heads were together like a pair of sweethearts who had been in love for months or even years.

Before long their whispering began to bother a lady two rows behind them. She kept glaring at them and saying "Shhh." Every time Jay turned and looked at her she glared and put her fingers to her lips, the hard line of her lips and the vertical line of her finger making the sign of a silent but unloving cross.

"We'd better be quiet," Ann said.

They tried that for a while, but Jay was bursting with explanations. Finally he couldn't take it anymore. "I'm going for some popcorn," he whispered. "Be right back." He stood up, walked out to the lobby, counted to ten, then turned around and walked ever so quietly back into the theater, slipping into an empty seat next to the lady behind them.

He leaned over and whispered to the lady as softly as he could, knowing how sharp Ann's hearing was. He enunciated very carefully so he could be understood the first time. He tried not to be nasty; after all the lady didn't know why they were talking so much.

"I'm sorry we're disturbing you, ma'am," Jay said. "I'm explaining the film to my friend because she's blind."

He stood up, walked back out to the lobby, and in a few minutes returned to Ann, with a giant tub of buttered popcorn.

"Hope our chewing isn't too noisy," he whispered, just loud enough that he might possibly be heard two rows back.

▶ Digging a little deeper:

Read I Samuel 16:1-13

A Touching Story

KEY VERSE ▶

"The Lord your God is with you, he is mighty to save. He will take great delight in you, he will quiet you with his love, he will rejoice over you with singing."

ZEPHANIAH 3:17

I'm telling you this because you don't know me. I wouldn't tell any of my friends or anyone who knows my friend Carrie. I'm not telling it because I'm a girl who likes to gossip, either; I am telling it because you might have a friend like Carrie too, someone who needs help. Or maybe it's happening to you.

It started in Mr. Landrud's class. He's one of my favorite teachers at Kennedy High. He's a hugger, but everyone thinks it's okay and he's okay. Like, one time after a test he came up beside me, put his arm around my shoulders, and gave me a little squeeze.

"You wrote the second best exam in class," he said, and smiled down at me. It was like Jesus paying me a compliment and giving me a squeeze.

Mr. Conklin—now that's a different story. He can look at some other girl across the gym floor and make *me* feel dirty. I wouldn't let him touch me. No way. But that's not the story.

Last spring, a couple of weeks before school let out, Mr. Landrud (the good hugger) put his hands on Carrie's shoulders, looked her in the eye, and said something nice about her contest essay. I watched her. She hardly heard the compliment. She just shriveled when he touched her. I couldn't understand it. If Mr. Conklin had touched me like that maybe, just maybe, I'd shrivel, but not if Mr. Landrud did.

I asked her about it out by our lockers. "I don't like men to touch me," she said.

"But he's so nice," I said.

"All men are dirty," she said.

That got me to thinking about Carrie and about some things my mom had told me. I should tell you about my mom. She's the greatest. We can talk about anything. And we do. We talk about stuff most kids wouldn't dare mention at home, like love and marriage and divorce, drugs, sex, stuff like that.

Well, anyhow, I got to thinking about Carrie, how she always used to want to spend the night with me or with somebody, anybody, anywhere but home. And how she used to hang around the locker room after gym class so she could take her shower alone, things like that. And when I was over at her house, her dad would sometimes act embarrassing. He touched her a lot. You couldn't tell by watching her, either, whether she liked it or not. I mean, you just couldn't tell. It was so weird. She just looked kind of bewildered and lost.

Anyway, I put this stuff together in my head and got to thinking, so I just asked her. You know me. No, you don't know me—but if you did, you'd know I'm always the one in class who asks the dumb question everyone else wants to ask, but doesn't dare. Or like, when some girlfriend seems to be avoiding me, I watch for her in the hallway, then I get on a crash course with her, and when our noses are about one foot apart I say, "What's wrong?"

That's what I did with Carrie. We were walking home together; no one around and we had plenty of time. This is what I said: "Is your dad doing stuff to you?"

She started to cry. We had to sit down on the Johnsons' rock wall. She cried and cried. I put my arm around her. "I knew it," I whispered in her ear.

"Who else knows?" she sobbed.

"I haven't told anyone," I said, "but you should."

"I couldn't."

"You have to." I paused a minute, then asked, "What does he do to you? Your father, I mean." Then she told me. The whole story. It just poured out. If my mom and I hadn't had all those talks, I would have freaked out right there on the sidewalk. Mom hadn't told me everything. I mean wow. Double wow. Her own father.

As I walked Carrie home after that, I began to think about the word father. I mostly call my father "Dad." The only time I hear the word "father" is when my mother is upset: "Your *father* will no doubt want to talk to you about this as well."

Where I hear the word "Father" all the time is in church: "God our Father," or, "Our Father, who art in heaven." God the Father is someone pretty neat to me, like my own father is most of the time, only better. But what does that word mean to someone like Carrie? I mean, where is her role model? I wouldn't want to think of God as father if I were her. I thought about that a lot and got angry inside. I tried not to hate her father, but it wasn't easy.

Next day after school I waited for her again. "Look," I said, "about yesterday . . ."

"I don't want to talk about it anymore."

"You have to. We have to. Come to my house. We'll talk to my mom. She'll know what to do."

Carrie wasn't all that easy to convince.

"You'll get my dad in trouble. All of us."

"You're already in trouble. What you need is someone to help you get out of it. Come on."

We went to my house and into the kitchen. It was my mom's day off. She was making bread and had flour all over her. As usual I just blurted it out. "Mom, Carrie and I need to talk to you. Her dad's been doing stuff to her. . . ."

That's how it started. We talked a long time, then my mom called Carrie's pastor. He came right over.

The bread didn't turn out very good. I guess Mom's heart wasn't into baking after what we went through with Carrie. No one in our family complained, though. I heard later that the school counselor got in on it, and a social service agency of Carrie's church, too.

That was last spring. Carrie stayed with her grandma all last summer. Since then we don't talk much anymore. We aren't the same kind of friends as we were. I think it's because I know something about her that she wishes no one knew, and that she wishes had never happened.

I'd do it again, though. It's hard to lose a friend, but it's better that she gets better.

It will take me a long time to forgive, I mean *really* forgive her father for doing that to her and to our friendship. If it takes *me* a long time, just think of how long it will take Carrie to forgive him. Will she ever? And will God ever be her Father? Ever? Wow.

▶ Digging a little deeper:

Read Genesis 19:30-38

The Runaway

KEY VERSE ▶   *"I will set out and go back to my father. . . ."*

LUKE 15:18

"John! I'm so relieved. Where have you been?"

"Just around. Stayed with some guys."

"It's been a week."

"I know."

"The police are looking for you, and the people at school. We all have been. Your parents are frantic."

"My mom, maybe."

"Your dad, too. And your brother."

"Not likely."

"Well, sit down a minute, and I'll call the police and tell them you're okay."

Pastor Quade studied John's face. There was the outline of a bruise on his left cheek. As the pastor began to dial the phone, John's face began to show mixed messages. He seemed glad to be found, but he obviously wasn't ready to go back. He didn't sit, but shuffled from one foot to another, his hands jammed into his jeans pockets. He glanced at the door several times as if he wanted to bolt back to the land of the lost.

Pastor Quade put the phone back down before it rang. "Don't you want me to call?" he asked.

"I don't know. I'm not ready to go home. If things stay the same, I'll never go home."

"What do you mean, the same?"

"With my dad."

"Nothing stays the same, and that includes your dad. At home it will get better or worse. It won't stay the same."

"It couldn't get much worse."

"I doubt that, but I can see how you might think so. Anyway, come sit down. I won't tie you to the chair."

John smiled faintly and sat at the corner of Pastor Quade's desk. The pastor rolled his office chair around the corner of the desk and they sat, facing each other, feet almost touching. John kept his eyes on their feet.

"I'd like to call the police," the pastor said. "Tell them you're with me and that you're okay. You are okay, aren't you?"

"Sure. I guess so."

"Can I call them?"

"I'll have to go home then, won't I?"

"You'll have to go somewhere."

"I'm not going home. Not yet."

"Supposing I were to promise that you won't have to go home until you're ready. Then could I call?"

John mused on that for a while.

"Well . . . could I?"

70

"I guess so," John finally said.

Pastor Quade had to look up the police station's business number again. He had decided on the earlier try not to dial 911. This was not a police emergency. As he paged through the phone book, he thought about his promise to John. He often made such broad and sweeping promises, promises that were sometimes hard to keep. They grew out of his natural hope and optimism. Like the time he told his entire youth group, "Whoever wants to go to Miami for the convention will go, I promise you that." Thirty–seven wanted to go. It cost a fortune. He dipped into their new car fund to help out. Kathy was furious.

"Hello. Hello. Yes. Could I talk to Lieutenant Ostlie?" There was a pause. "Hello, Dean? I've got John Wells here in my office. Yes. He's okay." Pause. "No, I'm not taking him home, at least not yet. Could you call his place and tell them he's all right? Maybe for now you shouldn't tell them where he is." Another pause. "Just say you've heard from him and he's okay. You can do that, can't you?" Pause. "Good."

Pastor Quade hung up the phone and sighed deeply. To think he could have gone into partnership with his uncle at the foundry and been managing it by now. He had thought about it before. At first it had seemed so simple, being in business. Then he thought of the trouble a business is bound to have sooner or later with staff and workers—and about the inevitable financial troubles, accounts receivable—unpaid bills—and then how he'd for sure have gotten hopelessly muddled in the lives of his foundry workers. He couldn't help meddling in people's lives. Friends had confided in him ever since he was in high school. Being a pastor, people expected him to be a meddler.

"So, John. What will we do with you?"

"I don't know."

"How did it start? What made you run?"

John began narrating, haltingly at first and then with more and more passion, the scene with his father and brother the week before. It had started Friday after school:

"My dad told both of us to come directly home from school on Friday because we were going to start painting the house. I came home as directly as I could, but Jim got there a half hour earlier than I did. That set my dad off."

"What delayed you?"

"Just a couple of conversations. One was with Miss Carvel. She wanted to talk about my last English essay. I couldn't very well say I wouldn't talk with her."

"And the other one?"

"Jennie. You know, Jennie Newberry. She was crying by her locker. There wasn't another soul in the hallway when I left Miss Carvel's office. Just Jenny and me. She was crying. I had to stop and see why."

"Did you try to explain that to your dad?"

"It would have helped. Usually if I just let him fuss a while, he gets over it. It would have worked, too, except for that ladder."

"That ladder?"

"It was windy Friday afternoon, and the ladder blew over."

"Was that so bad?"

"A gallon of brown paint was hanging on the ladder. It splattered all over the side of Dad's car—and not only that, the ladder landed across Mr. Fossum's spike picket fence and poked a hole in one rail. Dad didn't think it was safe to use."

"So you ruined the car and the ladder."

"I didn't. The wind did."

"Why didn't you move out of the wind?"

"Dad told us to start on the east side, away from the sun."

"So it was partly his fault that the ladder was on the windy side." Pastor Quade said it more as a suggestion than a question.

"I guess so, now that you mention it."

"How about the car?"

"It was latex paint. It washed off. But between washing the car and messing with the ladder and then going downtown to buy a new one, we didn't get much painting done."

"Sounds like a good plot for a Laurel and Hardy movie."

"My dad didn't think it was funny."

"No doubt. When did you run?"

"The next day. Dad was still upset on Saturday morning. We were behind schedule and it looked like rain and I got a couple of phone calls and he kept comparing Jim's painting to mine."

"And Jim's was better?"

"Sure. He's good at the fussy stuff. Takes him forever, but he's good. I just like to slap it on fast."

"Sounds like the two of you might make a good team."

"But Dad had us both doing the fussy stuff. Around the eaves and the corner trim. I was on the ladder, and he kept coming around and pointing and criticizing."

"Doesn't sound like you would have run away just for that." Pastor Quade kept sneaking glances at the bruise on John's cheek, knowing they had to get to that sooner or later.

"Finally Dad got so upset that he started up the ladder," John went on. "He doesn't like to climb, but being mad, I guess he forgot. 'Get off,' I said. 'Don't talk to me like that,' he said. 'Then get off,' I said, and started to shake the ladder. That reminded him where he was—ten feet off the ground. It scared him, I guess."

"And embarrassed him, too," Pastor Quade said. "Is that when he hit you?"

There was a long pause.

"When I came down," John said very softly, looking at his feet as he said it. Who wants to call his own father a child-abuser?

"Has he hit you before?"

Another long pause.

"You can tell me."

"He used to. A lot. When I was little. He never hit Jim. That made it worse. I hated Jim sometimes. Dad hadn't hit me for a long time, though. I thought the hitting was over. I guess that's why I ran. I dug out the money from my tax refund and just took off."

"Where did you stay?"

"Just around. With friends."

"So you didn't intend to leave town? To run away for real?"

"I guess not. I just needed to get away for a while."

"Your mom was terribly worried."

"I knew she would be."

"Your dad was too."

"I don't think so."

"Yes, he was. He blamed himself. I stopped over and he was terribly upset and nervous. He kept pacing the floor and asking Jim if you had said anything or hinted at anything."

"Jim is his little Mr. Perfect."

"He's older."

"It's not just that. He breaks his buns to please Mom and Dad."

"That's why your dad never had to hit him, I guess."

They both mused silently on that for a while.

"I'll tell you something about Jim," Pastor Quade said at last. "He's insecure. That's why he tries so hard to be right. Deep down, you probably are more sure of your parents' love than Jim is."

"Bull," John said. Then, realizing he was talking to his pastor, he put his hand over his mouth.

"It's not bull," Pastor Quade said, smiling. "You can goof off quite a bit, because you are free in your parents' love."

"My dad doesn't love me."

"He does. You'll see when you get home."

"Then why does he hit me?"

"That's a problem he's going to have to work out."

"Not on me, he isn't."

"I agree with that. But first we have to get you home. Let's call your house and negotiate a reentry."

"I don't know."

"Let me try."

"But you promised—"

"I remember. You can stay with Kathy and me tonight. Tomorrow, I'll call your house and we'll all five of us get together and talk."

"Okay," John said, reluctantly.

Another of his promises. *Kathy should love John, though,* Pastor Quade thought, *compared with Mike.* Mike came through town last December and moved in with them for over a week. He had ninety-proof breath and talked to himself constantly. Kathy didn't sleep much with Mike in the house.

"No more hitting," said John.

"Right. No more hitting."

Next morning Pastor Quade called the Wells home. Mr. Wells answered, first ring. The pastor explained the situation. After they had talked for a few minutes, he handed John the phone. "Here. Your dad wants to talk to you."

John hesitated a few moments, then said a tentative "Hello."

At that moment the whole episode looked to Pastor Quade like the story of the prodigal son. He watched John's face as he talked to his dad. Obviously a father's love, flawed though it was, was coming across town and through the wire. Somehow that love, short-circuited though it had been for many years, was invisibly caressing the bruised cheek and the bruised heart.

Mr. Wells was not a whole lot like the waiting father in the prodigal son story, Pastor Quade knew that. But he did love both his sons in his own way. There was enough love in that family, he thought, to begin putting things back together. The pastor figured it might be too big for him to handle alone, but he could refer them to family services counselors. Today was a good time enough to get started.

▶ Dig a little deeper:

Read Luke 15:11-32

Sylvia's Scissors

KEY VERSE ▶
*". . . Love does not insist on
its own way."*

I CORINTHIANS 13:5 (RSV)

Stan watched Sylvia kneeling in the grass on a late
autumn Sunday afternoon, eighty-five miles from her
home. She obviously didn't care about stains on her
dress or mud on her shoes. Tears were streaming down
her cheeks. No sobs. Just tears. It was five months too
late, but she was finally there at her grandfather's
graveside, saying good-bye. Stan felt privileged that
she had asked him to drive her to the cemetery. After
all, they were really just getting to know each other.

Sylvia took out a pair of dissecting scissors and
meticulously—and with what seemed to Stan a fierce
anger—trimmed the grass around her grandfather's
headstone as Stan looked on.

"Why did he have to die when I was an ocean
away?" she asked. The question demanded no answer.

Stan watched the scissors as she worked them
around the headstone. They were angled like the tape-

and-wrap scissors of an athletic trainer or an orthopedic nurse—except without the flattened lower jaw to slip under the tape.

The next time Sylvia pulled out those scissors was months later. They were walking across town toward the movie house on a Saturday night. It was only their third date. Stan had three stitches in his eyelid, a reminder of yesterday's soccer game. Every time he blinked, the tag end of one stitch dragged across his eyelid like a chipped tooth drags across the tongue.

"One of those stitches is really killing my eye," he said.

"Let's see." She pulled him under the streetlight. "Looks like Doc Walters left a long tail on one. Blink your eye."

Stan dutifully blinked.

"Sure. Every time you close your eye that stitch scrapes the lid."

"By the end of the movie I'll have a hole in my eyelid, by the way it feels."

"Probably not, but it will be irritated for sure."

"Clinic's closed now," he said.

"I can fix it." She dug in her jeans pocket and pulled out the scissors, which she waggled in front of his nose. "I've cut up a lot of frogs with these."

"You washed them since?"

"Do you want to go find a doctor, or do you want it fixed?"

"Just fix it. We'll be late for the show."

She tipped his head back to look. "Light's not good enough," she pronounced, looking up into the streetlight. She looked around, considering options. "See if the door on that car is open."

Stan reluctantly tried the door on a parked car. "It's open."

"Well, reach in and turn on the lights."

"We don't even know whose car it is."

"Just turn them on. It won't take a minute."

Stan cautiously turned on the lights and eased the door back into its first notch. When he turned, Sylvia was sitting on the curb, three feet in front of the car's right-hand headlight.

"Lie down on your back and put your head on my knee, right here in the light." She patted her knee to show him just where she wanted him.

Quickly she snipped the stitch and pushed him off her knee. Before he was even back on his feet, she had turned off the car lights and slammed the door, loudly. "I could save you a fortune with these scissors," she chortled, brushing the dust off his back.

Stan looked nervously over his shoulder to see if anyone had been watching.

An hour later, in the balcony of the Grand Theater, Stan decided he really liked this impetuous girl. Impulsively, acting on his decision, he leaned across to kiss her on the lips.

Sylvia whipped out her scissors, brandished them in front of his nose in the flashing silver light of the big screen, and with a mock snarl said, "Do that again or I'll stab you."

"Did you say *and* or *or*?" He really wasn't sure he had heard right. Her face betrayed nothing.

"I said *or*."

He leaned across and kissed her again. Being ready for it this time, she kissed him back. In the flickering light of the screen, her face showed the smile lines in her cheeks and at the corners of her eyes.

"Do that to anyone else and I'll clip you like Samson," she whispered in his ear, running the scissors up his back and into his hair.

The scissors soon became a reminder of many things they had done together: opening birthday cards, cutting and pasting research papers, standing in her mother's garden clipping altar flowers for church.

As he sat beside her in church one morning, Stan thought about Sylvia's scissors. They were a perfect symbol of how a relationship ought to work: two knives pinned to each other to work together, their cutting edges side by side, not cutting each other but working together, not able to cut anything at all unless they worked in concert.

"Faith is the pin," he said, right in the middle of the sermon.

"Shh," said Sylvia.

Faith in God and in each other, he thought. *Faith is the pin, the hinge.*

"What were you mumbling about during the sermon?" she asked afterwards.

"Nothing, really. Just don't lose your scissors."

▶ Dig a little deeper:

Read I Corinthians 13

Helping Grandpa Die

KEY VERSE ▶

". . . Though outwardly we are wasting away, yet inwardly we are being renewed day by day."

II CORINTHIANS 4:16

Last week I watched my Grandpa Ted die. Day by day, hour by hour, he died. He was in our downstairs bedroom for three weeks. Two nurses came, a woman in the morning and a man in the evening. They washed him, turned him, and gave him shots. His room smelled weird. We all smelled it. The whole house smelled worse and worse as Grandpa got sicker and sicker, but no one complained. I once heard someone say, "We don't speak ill of the dead." That means the dying, too, I guess. Even if they smell.

What I couldn't believe was what happened to my father. He isn't a very warm man, my dad. I can't even remember the last time he hugged me. But things changed quickly just before Grandpa died.

Wednesday before school, Grandpa Ted called to Dad and then Dad called me in from my breakfast in the kitchen.

"Grandpa wants to see how you've grown. Turn around."

Dad and I stood back to back as we had done for Grandpa many times recently—and as my sister, Amy, and I had done for years. The back of my head fit into the curve in the back of my father's head. He was still half a head taller.

"See, Pop, how big he's getting?" Father said to Grandpa. He talked as if I were a five year old. We just stood there for a minute and looked down on Grandpa. He seemed to have shrunk just in the last three weeks.

Grandpa whispered in his grating voice, "Good for you, Mark. Good for you."

I leaned over and kissed him on the cheek. "I have to get ready for school now, Gramps. See you later."

"Maybe yes, maybe no," he rasped. I saw tears in my father's eyes as I was leaving.

I spent a normal day in school, and when I got home, Grandpa was much worse. He could barely see me. I whispered in his ear, and his eyes moved. He knew I was there.

Thursday morning when I got up, Gramps wasn't even awake.

"He's slipped into a coma," Mom whispered. Dad was sitting on a chair, holding one of Grandpa's hands and staring into space.

I sat there and thought, oddly enough, about coma and comma. If all of life is like a sentence, then maybe a coma is the comma that moves us on to the next part, the heaven part, to make the sentence complete.

The nurse came, took Grandpa's pulse, lifted his eyelids and looked in, then picked up his other hand and shouted into his ear, "Mr. Gates, can you hear me? Squeeze my hand." She repeated it three times, then looked at my father and shook her head. I've never seen Dad look so sad.

Out in the hallway, Mom and the nurse talked. "How long will it be?" my mother asked her.

"It's always hard to say, Mrs. Gates. Could be today; could be tonight. Maybe even tomorrow."

My father stepped out of the room. "Is there anything we should do?" he asked.

"Talk to him," she said. "Who knows what he can hear? Some folks I worked with last month used to record their dinner conversation, then play the tape off and on all day in their grandma's room. It must be nice to die with the voices of people you love around you."

"What a wonderful idea," my mother said.

"It's too late for that now," my father whispered. "But I'll stay with him."

"I could stay home from school," I offered, perhaps too eagerly.

"No," Dad said. "You go this morning. We'll see at lunchtime. Come home for lunch today, will you?"

I nodded.

"And Jane," he said to Mom, "you'd better go to work. This is your monthly sales meeting day, isn't it?"

She nodded. "Call if there's any change," she said.

The nurse left. Amy came down from upstairs, and

my mother gathered us all in Grandpa's room. "Would you say a prayer for Grandpa, Amy?"

"I guess so," she said.

"Come over here and say it loud," Father said. "He may be able to hear us."

Amy prayed for Grandpa Ted and for us all. She asked that God would teach us to love each other while there was still time. She was saying something important with that prayer. Neat girl, my sister.

When she finished, Mom and Dad hugged us, both of us, and we left for school. Think of it. A hug from dad. Call it sudden answer to prayer if you like.

In school that morning, I thought about death. Does death make people love each other more? Does death make life worth more, make people care more? Is that why Jesus had to die? To make people more valuable to God and to each other?

I went home at noon, slipped in the back door, and put my books on the kitchen table. I brought everything home just in case I didn't go back. I walked into Grandpa's room, and my dad was sitting on the bed with Grandpa's head in his lap. He seemed only slightly embarrassed about it. Grandpa was breathing in gasps, about every three or four seconds.

"Aren't you afraid you'll hurt him?" I asked.

"What could hurt him now?" Dad said. "Sit down and hold his hand for a while."

"I'll go to the bathroom first."

When I came back and sat down, I took Grandpa's frail hand in both of my own. His skin was like paper. I took up a little of it between my thumb and forefinger.

Like parchment, and blotchy with blood spots underneath.

"Would you sing for him?" Dad asked.

"Like what?"

"I don't know. He used to sing 'I Need Thee Every Hour' quite a bit."

"I don't know the words."

"Go get his old hymnbook off the piano."

I put Grandpa's hand back on the bed and went and got the book. I found the hymn and laid the book open on the bed. I sang. Dad hummed along. I looked up at Dad when I was finished. Tears were streaming down his cheeks.

"I never told him I loved him," he whispered. He didn't say it to me exactly. Maybe he just needed to say it out loud. But I responded anyway.

"Wouldn't he know that you loved him without your saying it?" I asked.

"I guess so. But why do we wait so long?"

"I don't know. Why don't you shout it into his ear? If he can hear the hymn, maybe he can hear that, too."

"I LOVE YOU!" Dad yelled it first, then he said it. "I love you." Then he whispered it. "I love you." The third time was more for himself than for Gramps. Even before he got sick, Gramps wouldn't have heard that whisper. But I heard it. Maybe it was also for me.

Then a strange thing happened. Dad turned to me, stared me straight in the eye and said, "Well, listen to this, Mark Adam Gates, my only begotten son. I love you." He smiled as he said it. It was something to see, I tell you, him sitting there smiling, tears running down his cheeks, holding gasping old Gramps.

"I love you too, Dad," I said. Now there were tears running down *my* cheeks.

Love and death.

Grandpa died about a half hour later. The time between breaths just got longer and longer until he just plain didn't take the next one. Love and death.

I guess the smell in our house will go away in a while. Some other things will stay behind, though. Memories, mostly. I'm glad I was home with my dad, to help my grandpa die.

▶ Dig a little deeper:

Read II Corinthians 4:16—5:10

The Parable of the Father and Son

KEY VERSE ▶

"And we know that in all things God works for the good of those who love him, who have been called according to his purpose."

ROMANS 8:28

"Hi, Pastor. Out for a walk?"

"Hi, Bill. Yeah. I'm getting too chubby. Got to walk it off. Hey, I saw your picture in the paper."

"Yeah? Whadja think, Pastor?"

"You looked like a movie star."

"No, I mean the interview. What about that?"

"You gave some interesting answers. I learned some things about you. Like, I didn't know you wanted to be an engineer."

"I do."

"And your hobby is windsurfing."

"Yup."

"At least you didn't say your hobby was girls."

"It isn't."

"Carla wishes she were your hobby."

"I'd rather windsurf."

"I know. She does hang around you a lot at youth

group, though."

"She drives me nuts."

"She's a nice girl, Bill."

"I suppose so."

"But you'd rather windsurf, right?"

"I'd rather do almost anything else."

Pastor Shurman thought back over Bill's last several years. Bill's father had died, and an uncle, too, and a younger sister had been hit by a car and died painfully, horribly. They had been through a lot, Bill's family. He had been through a lot—a frightful lot for someone his age.

"One of your most interesting answers during the interview," the pastor said, "was who you would like to talk to from the past."

"You mean Jesus?"

"Yes. A lot of kids would have picked a baseball hero like Babe Ruth, or a president, or an adventurer like Charles Lindbergh. Yours was a special kind of response. What would you ask Him?"

"Jesus, you mean?"

"Yeah. If you could have Him here on the street corner with us for a half hour."

"I don't know. What God's like, I guess—and what heaven's like."

"That stuff's in the Bible," the pastor said. "You must have more personal things to ask."

"I guess I do. I'd ask about my dad, I think, and my sister. I wonder if they're happy over there."

"Do you believe they're with God?"

"I want to believe that."

"They had strong faith, both of them. Your father didn't talk about it much, but it was there."

"Why did they have to die?" Bill said slowly.

"Is that one of the questions you would ask Jesus?"

"Yeah, I guess it is. I'd like to know that. I really would." There was an edge to Bill's voice now, almost like anger. His suffering wasn't over yet, the pastor could see, not by a long way.

Pastor Shurman could also see that Bill was getting nervous. This wasn't easy for him, talking about feelings. "You know what I think, Bill? I think if you could ask Jesus a question like that, He wouldn't give you a straight answer."

"You mean He wouldn't know?"

"No. I don't mean that. It's just that too much truth isn't always good for us. Or too much truth too easily—or too soon. He wants us to struggle for our answers."

"I sure haven't found any answers for that one yet. And it hasn't been easy, either."

"I'm sure it hasn't. You may never get a complete answer. You may never know for sure. Jesus would probably put it to you in a parable."

"A parable?"

"You know, a little story. Like 'The Prodigal Son' or 'The Good Samaritan.' "

"What kind of story would he tell about a father dying of cancer and a sister on a bicycle, hit by a drunk driver?"

"I don't know. That would be a tough one. Maybe it would be two stories. The father-son one might be an adventure story. A father and a son, shepherds let's say, out with the flock. A lion attacks. The father says to the boy, 'Run home for help.' When they get back, the father has been killed."

"Not a very pleasant story. What's the point?"

"Maybe the father died for the the son. Saves him."

"You think my father died for me?"

"It may turn out that way. Are you a different person than you were before your father got sick?"

"I suppose I am. I work a lot more."

"Around home, you mean?"

"Yeah. And my mom depends on me more."

"Maybe that kind of responsibility will be good for you in the long run. Maybe even save you from something."

There was a long silence. Bill finally said, "That was too big a price to pay."

"I know. Jesus paid it too. It all has something to do with love. You could also ask about that."

"Yeah."

"You coming to youth group tomorrow?" Pastor Shurman could see that the conversation was coming to an end, and he wanted to give Bill an out.

"I plan to be there," he said.

"Should I save you a place next to Carla?"

"Ha," Bill said, running off with a wave.

Nice kid, the pastor thought. *That's one thing I'd like to ask Jesus about, too. Why does a nice kid like Bill have to lose both his father and his sister?* He shook his head, then looked down at how his belly was pooching out between the buttonholes on his shirt. He'd better continue his walk.

▶ **Dig a little deeper:**

I Thessalonians 4:13-18

An Interview with the Author

Why stories for a devotional book, Steve? Why not regular devotions with discussions and prayers?

You could ask the same question of Jesus. He was—and is—the Son of God. He knew all truth absolutely. So why did He tell stories? Simply, He told stories to teach truths. Jesus knew all about heaven. But when He wanted to teach His disciples about heaven, He told them the stories of the the lost coin, the lost sheep, and the mustard seed. When He wanted to teach them about love, He made up the story of the good Samaritan.

Why were the stories more effective than a straight answer?

Because nothing catches our interest like a story. A

story stimulates our imagination and helps us picture ourselves in a similar situation. That's how we learn from it.

So maybe, if we've listened to a story, we'll remember what we learned when someday a similar situation happens to us?

That's right. For instance, if I were a teenager, I think I'd rather learn some truths about abortion by reading a story about abortion than by going through that devastating experience with my best friend. But if my best friend were to get into trouble someday, maybe the story I'd read would help me make better and more helpful suggestions to my friend.

A story is also bendable. In our imaginations we can mold it so that its narrative fits more exactly the situations we know about. We can say, "That's kind of like what happened to Sarah." Or maybe even more important, "That could happen to me. I'd better watch out."

What do you want this book to accomplish, Steve?

These are stories about relationships—the "bridges" we build to other people. Being a teenager has always been hard, and it's getting harder by the year. I think teens need all the help they can get as they try to learn better ways of relating to their peers—classmates, teammates, best friends, sweethearts—and to their authority figures—parents, teachers, pastors—and to God.

I hope that reading these stories will make kids think about the role God and others play in the stories of their own lives, and about the bridges they are building or tearing down every day. I hope it will remind them that a lot of wonderful people are out there ready to help if they'll just say the word—Christian friends, teachers, pastors, counselors, parents, friends' parents. And I hope the kids who read these stories will be motivated to turn again and again to the best and most faithful helpers of all: God, Jesus His Son, and their Holy Spirit.